CAST IN ORDER OF APPEARANCE

Father Joseph Mitchell

Cyprian Akuta

Father Zachary Azuka

The Most Reverend Maurice FitzMaurice,
    Bishop of Abuka

Father Anthony O'Brien

Sister Eileen

Mother Gertrude

Gregory Olume

*The action of the play takes place in the priests'
house in Uzala, Eastern Nigeria, during the years
1967 to 1970.*

[3]

AUTHOR'S PREFACE

The mission of Uzala in Eastern Nigeria is entirely imaginary and so are all the people who pass in and out through its ever-open doorway. But the events which form the background to the story were only too real.

Towards the end of 1966 the smouldering tribal hatreds of Nigeria burst into flames. The principal vicitims were the members of the Ibo tribe, who were massacred in thousands in many parts of the Federation of Nigeria. Fearing genocide, the Ibos decided to leave the Federation and in May 1967 they declared the Eastern Region of Nigeria to be an independent state, the Republic of Biafra.

The Federal Government were determined to maintain the unity of Nigeria, if necessary by force. Fighting soon began and the war dragged on for two and a half years, ending with the surrender of what was left of Biafra in January 1970.

There were many casualties as a result of the fighting but even more as a result of starvation and disease. The conscience of the world was stirred by pictures of starving children in beleaguered Biafra and a massive relief airlift was mounted by the Red Cross and the Churches, flying every night from the islands of Sao Tomé and Fernando Po to the Biafran airstrip at Uli.

Much of the work of administering relief within Biafra was done by Irish missionary priests and nuns, often at great risk to themselves. Their work helped to save millions of lives but may also have prolonged Biafra's will to fight. That was the view taken by the Federal Government which after the war arrested and deported the missionaries still remaining in the former Biafra. The fears of genocide, however, proved quite unfounded and the Government pursued a policy of reconciliation with the Ibos that has helped to heal the scars of civil war more quickly than anyone could have foreseen.

The missionaries are in some ways the saddest victims of the war. Because they had the misfortune to be on the losing side of the front line, they are shut out for ever from the land to which they had given their hearts and lives. To them this play is dedicated with respect and affection.

ACT ONE

The scene is the priests' house in a Catholic mission in east-
ern Nigeria. On the left, a verandah, raised one step above the
ground, runs in front of the bedroom wing of the bungalow. A
door leads from it to the living room, which occupies the right
hand side of the stage. The front wall of the living room has been
removed so that we can see its interior. It is furnished in rather
spartan fashion with a dining table and chairs, a sideboard, a
wooden bench and a refrigerator. On the walls hang a crucifix
and a few pictures, including Pope Paul VI and the Bishop of
Abuka. Doors lead to the bedrooms and to the kitchen.

There are a few battered basket chairs on the verandah. On
one of them is seated Father Joe Mitchell as the play begins. He
is a man of about fifty, wearing lightweight trousers or shorts,
open-necked shirt and sandals. A newspaper in a wrapper lies
beside him on the floor.

MITCHELL [*Shouts without moving his head*]: Cyprian! [*No*
   answer.] Cyprian!
   [*Cyprian enters, carrying a clean white soutane. He is an*
   Ibo youth of about eighteen, wearing a plain shirt and shorts.]
CYPRIAN: Yes, Father.
MITCHELL: Cyprian, what was it I wanted?
CYPRIAN: Your soutane, Father. The bishop is coming.
MITCHELL: No, that wasn't it. I know. The newspapers from
   home. What did you do with them?
CYPRIAN: They are here, Father.
MITCHELL: Thanks. You know, I have a silver-haired old mother
   in the County of Mayo who sends me the Sunday papers
   every week. She sits beside the turf fire in the gloaming
   [*Struggles with wrapper.*], wearing her fingers to the bone,
   plastering yards and yards of sticky tape all over them so
   that the bloody light-fingered Nigerians won't be able to pinch
   the sporting section. No offence meant. [*He catches his nail.*]
   Damn!
CYPRIAN: I take no offence. I am not a Nigerian.
MITCHELL: You could have fooled me.

[5]

CYPRIAN: I am an Ibo man. I am a Biafran.

MITCHELL [*Wearily*]: Here we go again. Sit down Cyprian. [*Cyprian sits on the step of the verandah.*] Now, repeat after me: I am a member of the Ibo tribe. [*No answer.*] Well, you are, aren't you?

CYPRIAN: I am an Ibo man.

MITCHELL: I am also a citizen of Nigeria.

CYPRIAN [*Sullenly*]: No, Father.

MITCHELL: You're really taking this thing seriously.

CYPRIAN: Yes, Father.

MITCHELL: There is no such place as Biafra. Is not, was not, and never will be. Look, I know you've had a raw deal. But you'll never go it alone. The Federal Government have an army and they'll use it.

CYPRIAN: We will have an army too. An army of Ibo men.

MITCHELL: I'm sure you will. And it'll be the best organised army in Africa. You'll have a commander-in-chief and a general staff and a whole platoon of quartermasters, typing out requisitions in triplicate for elastic-sided Balaclava helmets. The only thing you won't have is fighting men. If the Ibos are a nation, which I don't for a moment admit, they're a nation of shopkeepers.

[*Father Zachary Azuka enters while he is still speaking. He is an Ibo priest in his mid-thirties, intelligent, soft-spoken, dressed in a clean white soutane.*]

ZACHARY: I thought it was the Irish who were the nation of shopkeepers.

MITCHELL: Actually, it was the English, if you really want to know.

ZACHARY: It's nothing to be ashamed of. Every nation needs shopkeepers. It goes with civilization. It was the Irish who taught us to be shopkeepers, just as they taught us to be Christians.

MITCHELL: Go and get chop ready, Cyprian, please.

CYPRIAN: Yes, Father. [*He goes, leaving soutane behind.*]

ZACHARY: It was the Irish also who taught us the idea of nationhood—

MITCHELL: Your nation is Nigeria—

ZACHARY: Who taught us that nationhood depends on the heart

[6]

and will of a people, not on boundaries drawn on a map by British colonialists. Every dead Empire leaves its monuments behind. The British boundaries are like the Roman roads, striding across the landscape in dead straight lines, neither knowing nor caring about the people they pass through.

MITCHELL: There's no analogy between Ireland and what's going on here. This isn't nationalism, it's just tribalism.

ZACHARY: One man's tribe is another man's nation.

MITCHELL: I don't know what to say. I used to feel I could talk to your people, even if I didn't know very much of the language. But now I don't seem to be getting through any more.

ZACHARY: That's what all parents say about their children when they start to grow up.

MITCHELL: I'm not treating you like children.

ZACHARY: All parents say that too.

MITCHELL: Well, why do you behave like children? Why do you drift into civil war without raising a finger to stop yourselves?

ZACHARY: Because it is our destiny. We must fight for our freedom as you fought for yours.

MITCHELL: It's not the same thing.

ZACHARY: Why? Is there any reason why your freedom is worth fighting for and ours is not? Is it because you are white and we are black?

MITCHELL: That's the trouble with all of you. You're so bloody sensitive. You find racial implications in every remark.

ZACHARY: I find them because they are there.

MITCHELL: What time is the bishop coming?

ZACHARY: Any time now.

MITCHELL: Why is he coming?

ZACHARY: He is bringing the new priest.

MITCHELL: Anyone could have brought the new priest. He must have some other reason for coming.

ZACHARY: You'd better put on your soutane.

MITCHELL: Why should I put on my soutane?

ZACHARY: Don't put it on, then.

[*Mitchell puts on his soutane, then goes to the sideboard and pours himself a drink of whiskey.*]

[7]

MITCHELL: And I'd better not have whiskey on my breath, either. [*Drinks.*] Not with my reputation. The curse of the Irish. You drink-um white man's fire-water?

ZACHARY: No, thank you. I think I hear a car.

MITCHELL: Where are my sweets?

ZACHARY: Did you try your pockets?

MITCHELL [*Taking peppermints from pocket*]: Brilliant! Who said black men were less intelligent than white men? [*Puts sweet in his mouth.*] And so, smelling sweetly but suspiciously of peppermint, he awaits the arrival of his lord and master, the Most Reverend Maurice FitzMaurice, Bishop of Abukaba and the biggest pain in the pelvis in West Africa. Is my smile wide enough? [*He leers at Zachary.*]

ZACHARY: Too wide, I think.

MITCHELL [*Without removing leer*]: Infossivle!

[*He goes to the verandah, followed by Zachary. The bishop comes up on to the verandah, followed by Father Anthony O'Brien and Cyprian, carrying two cases, which he takes away to a bedroom. The bishop, aged about seventy, wears a white soutane and gold chain and cross. O'Brien wears a white soutane, and is also wearing glasses.*]

BISHOP [*Shaking hands*]: Hello, Father. Hello, Father.

MITCHELL: You're very welcome to our mission here at Uzala. It may not be the brightest jewel in Bishop FitzMaurice's mitre, but I think you'll like it very well. Sit down, take the weight off your feet. Anyone for a drink? [*They sit on verandah chairs.*] Father O'Brien?

O'BRIEN: I'll have a beer, please. [*Zachary goes to fridge, pours out beers.*]

MITCHELL: My Lord, would you like a drop of the hard stuff? [*Goes to sideboard.*]

BISHOP: No, thanks. I'll have a beer too. I think whiskey is a drink for the evening.

MITCHELL: An excellent drink for the evening. [*Pours himself whiskey.*] Well, My Lord, here's mud in your episcopal eye.

BISHOP: Sláinte.

O'BRIEN: Cheers.

[*All are now seated, Mitchell with a glass of whiskey, the other three with glasses of beer.*]

[8]

MITCHELL: Well, now, Father O'Brien—

O'BRIEN: Call me Tony.

MITCHELL: Well, Tony, does Nigeria live up to your expectations?

O'BRIEN: Yes, pretty much what I expected. I was a bit surprised at the barriers, though.

MITCHELL: Barriers?

BISHOP: Yes, they've started putting up road-blocks along all the main roads, kind of military check-points.

MITCHELL: That's interesting.

BISHOP: A rather curious thing happened yesterday to two of the sisters. These soldiers stopped their car at a road-block and told them to get out and to take off their veils and their shoes. Well, one of the sisters happened to be Mother Gertrude— [*To O'Brien.*] You'll be meeting her shortly—

MITCHELL: Otherwise known as Galloping Gertie.

BISHOP: Of course, when they saw it was Gertrude they were terrified, but they still stuck to their story. They said they had strict orders to search all shoes and hats. Eventually, after a bit of palaver, the lieutenant produced a letter from Headquarters which said that soldiers at road-blocks were to stop all cars and to search their boots and bonnets. Boots and bonnets, do you get it? [*They do.*] Gertrude wasn't at all amused. She told the lieutenant he was an ignorant waster and she knew his father before him and he was an ignorant waster too.

MITCHELL: All the same it's looking serious.

BISHOP: My information is that the formal declaration of independence is expected within the next twenty-four hours. By tomorrow night we will be living in the Republic of Biafra. I was in Enugu over the weekend and they showed me some of the preparations. They've got a flag and a national anthem ready and the government printing press is turning out stamps and banknotes by the million.

MITCHELL: God, but you couldn't be up to them!

BISHOP [*Smoothly*]: Father Zachary, we appreciate all that the Ibo people have suffered. I was explaining to Father Tony on the way here that there are faults on both sides.

ZACHARY: We Ibos are a difficult people, Father O'Brien. When we are hurt, we cry out. When we are wounded, we bleed.

[9]

When we are attacked, we defend ourselves.

MITCHELL: "Hath not a Jew eyes? Hath not a Jew hands, organs, dimensions, senses, affections, passions?"

BISHOP: The Ibos have in fact been compared to the Jews. Their very success has tended to make them unpopular, without cause, largely.

ZACHARY: When they told us that Nigeria was one country, we believed them and went south and west and north. When they told us the country needed building up, we tried to build it up. We educated ourselves, we worked hard, we became shopkeepers and doctors and teachers and civil servants and priests. The whole of Nigeria was run by Ibos because the other tribes were too stupid or too lazy to do anything themselves. They envied us and they hated us and they decided to destroy us. Will I tell you about it, Father O'Brien?

O'BRIEN: If you wouldn't mind.

ZACHARY: I was teaching in a junior seminary in the Northern Region. There were five Ibos altogether on the staff and twenty-one among the boys. There was no moon that night. I had gone into the town to post a letter and that is what saved my life. On the way back I saw lights outside the school and heard noise but it wasn't until I was quite near that I could see what was going on. They had brought out all the Ibos into the quadrangle in front of the main building and they were killing them one by one. With knives. Not very quickly. I turned around and ran into the bush. One or two of them saw me and followed me but not for long. They were too drunk to run very well and anyhow they didn't want to miss the fun. I kept on running and running and for a long time I could hear the screams coming from the school. Then at last I couldn't hear them any more, whether because they had stopped or because I was too far away, I don't know. They killed all the twenty-five Ibos in the school that night. One of them was my brother. [*Pause.*]

BISHOP: The word "brother" in Africa is used rather loosely of any kind of relative. It's rather like the Old Testament. You remember Abraham and Lot—

ZACHARY: Twenty-five Ibos and one of them was my brother. Over the whole country they killed thirty thousand Ibos and all of them were my brothers.

BISHOP: We're only re-opening old wounds, reviving old hatreds.

ZACHARY: We are Christians. We do not hate anyone. All we ask is to left alone to go our own way in peace.

BISHOP: Peace! Blessed peace! Is it not what we are all seeking, each in his own way?

O'BRIEN [*Finishing beer*]: Amen.

BISHOP [*Rising*]: Father Zachary, could I have a few words with you in your room?

ZACHARY: Yes, My Lord.

BISHOP: After you. [*They go off into the house.*]

MITCHELL: He. Is. Up. To. Something. He has a dagger up that well-filled sleeve and it will be decorating somebody's shoulder-blades before the day is out. I know the signs of old.

O'BRIEN: You're rather hard on him. I think he's quite a deecnt sort.

MITCHELL: A bishop is supposed to be the centre of unity in his diocese and our bishop certainly is. Everybody hates him.

O'BRIEN: Oh, come on, you don't hate him.

MITCHELL: I love him as I love all mankind. But it's a strictly theological kind of love. I've known him for a long time— he was my Dean of Studies at school—and I've had plenty of time to hone my prejudices to a sharp cutting edge.

O'BRIEN: He was telling me that this was one of the first missions in Eastern Nigeria.

MITCHELL: Tactfully changing the subject. Yes, it was founded in the early twenties. Mother Gertrude has been here almost from the beginning. She'll tell you all about the history of the place if you want to know. She's part of the history of the place herself. In fact, she's part of the history of Nigeria. As tough as an old crocodile and just about as lovable.

MITCHELL: Do you know that she was the one who introduced into Nigeria the supreme emblem of all that is best and finest in the traditions of the Irish convent school?

O'BRIEN: Which is?

MITCHELL: Don't rush me, it's not often I get a new audience. Picture Nigeria as it was in those benighted days, a land darkened by idolatry and superstition, a land of primitive lust and pagan passion. But help is at hand. Somewhere a light is beginning to shine in the darkness. Up the river from the coast strange objects are being ferried, great mysterious parcels bearing the simple inscription "Mother Gertrude, Uzala Mission, Eastern Nigeria." Faithful native bearers are waiting at the landing stage to receive the precious burdens, and to carry them through trackless jungles and snake-infested swamps, fighting off lions and tigers and hostile tribesmen, until at length they reach the little convent at Uzala. On the steps of the school they undo their corded bales and reveal the contents. There they lie in neatly ribboned piles, their Clery's labels gleaming white in the sunlight: two hundred and fifty pairs of heavy-duty navy-blue nether garments, females for the use of. In a word, knickers.

O'BRIEN: Two hundred and fifty pairs?

MITCHELL: Two hundred and fifty pairs. It was the beginning of civilization as we know it in Eastern Nigeria. What the maidens of Uzala wore beneath their dresses before that day, if they wore anything, is lost in the mists of pre-history. But from that day onward they were solid cotton from the navel to the knee. Gertrude imposed a real reign of terror. She became the Robespierre of Uzala, the navy-blue incorruptible. There were surprise inspections, drumhead court-martials, summary convictions. Any girl who was tried and found wanting was out of the school and back in her village within the hour. Draconian measures, but they worked. From Uzala a great surge of navy-blue morality swept out like a tidal wave over the whole of Eastern Nigeria. It was Gertrude's finest hour and it made her an institution, a national monument. Even today, nearly fifty years later, whenever she walks through Uzala market-place, aged grandmothers clutch their skirts in panic and disappear behind grass-huts.

O'BRIEN: How many sisters are there in the convent now?

MITCHELL: Do you mean European sisters or African sisters?

O'BRIEN: I just mean sisters.

MITCHELL: There are two Irish sisters, Gertrude and Eileen, and four Ibo sisters.

O'BRIEN: That makes six sisters. [*Mitchell raises eyebrows.*] Two and four makes six.

MITCHELL: Forgive me, but am I missing some delicate nuance?

[12]

O'BRIEN: It's not anything really.

MITCHELL: No, please tell me. I'd like to know.

O'BRIEN: It's just the automatic distinction between Irish sisters and Ibo sisters. Africans are people too.

MITCHELL: That's very good. Only a week here and you've noticed that already.

O'BRIEN: I know what I want to say and I know that when I try to say it it's going to come out all wrong and big-headed. I've only been a week in Nigeria and you've been here for twenty-five years but because I'm new I can notice things that you don't.

MITCHELL: Fire ahead, I'm listening.

O'BRIEN: We were taught that the job of the missionary is to work himself out of his job. Right?

MITCHELL: Go on.

O'BRIEN: His job is to build up the local church so that it is self-sufficient, so that it doesn't need missionaries any more. The hard thing is to judge when that time has come, when— to take our own case—the Irish should clear out and leave it to the Ibos to run their own show.

MITCHELL: You think we should go now?

O'BRIEN: I don't know. I'm not here long enough to know.

MITCHELL: When you've been here as long as I have, you'll know.

O'BRIEN: That's exactly what I'm afraid of. At the moment I feel I may be dispensable. But after I've been here twenty-five years, I will be quite certain I'm indispensable.

MITCHELL: I don't think I'm personally indispensable. But I know that the Church couldn't survive here without the white missionaries.

O'BRIEN: How do you know until you've tried? That's the argument the colonial powers used. They said the Africans weren't ready to govern themselves.

MITCHELL: And maybe they were right. Look at this damn country. Only barely independent and it's about to have a civil war.

O'BRIEN: You'll have to admit, Joe, that we Irish are hardly in a position to throw stones. You don't mind me calling you Joe?

MITCHELL: Not in the least.

[13]

O'BRIEN: Would you mind if Zachary called you Joe?

MITCHELL [*After a slight pause*]: He wouldn't. The question doesn't arise.

O'BRIEN: I know it doesn't. That's one of the things that worries me.

MITCHELL: It doesn't worry me. And I don't think it worries them.

O'BRIEN [*Musingly*]: Them.

MITCHELL: Third person plural of the pronoun. It's the only form I know. Look, we'll continue ths discussion later—say twelve months' time? Another beer? [*Bishop and Zachary return.*] Or would you like to try some of our palm wine? It's quite good. Don't mind the bishop. He believes in supporting local industries, isn't that so, My Lord?

BISHOP: Indeed. [*To O'Brien.*] I think it's time you went over to see the sisters. Zachary will bring you across. I'll follow you over in a few minutes. Yes.

MITCHELL: We'll keep the palm wine till you get back.

ZACHARY: This way, Father. [*Zachary and O'Brien go out.*]

BISHOP [*With forced heartiness*]: Well, Father Joe, and how is the heart keeping up?

MITCHELL: The heart? Do you mean the physical organ itself, or the complex of emotions, passions and affections for which it is popularly supposed to stand?

BISHOP: I find it a little bit hard to follow you sometimes.

MITCHELL: I'm sorry, I didn't mean to be difficult. I'm sure I can be very tiresome at times.

BISHOP: So can we all, Father, so can we all. We are all human, even bishops. The other day I had a fellow in from the Ministry of Education, a very officious type, asking a lot of stupid questions about our school building programme. And then, do you know, the thought came to me: this chap here is annoying me, but how do I know that I am not annoying him? That's something that doesn't often strike one. I said to myself, this chap has his own problems, just as I have mine. His soul has the same value in the sight of God as mine, practically. That's why we must all bear with one another's weaknesses. On the way here I passed a crippled man on the road. One hand was holding a stick, the other

[14]

was on the shoulder of a little girl, a slip of a thing, she might have been his granddaughter. And I thought to myself: Life is like that. Yes, I said to myself, Life is like that. There is no one so strong but needs some help, no one so weak but has some help to offer. Yes, I said to myself, Life's like that.

MITCHELL: That's very true. [*Slight pause.*] Was there something—?

BISHOP: Yes. Yes, indeed. I have rather an important piece of news and I wanted you to be the first to know, almost. You see, I've offered my resignation and it's been accepted.

MITCHELL: You've resigned? As bishop?

BISHOP: Yes. I shall be going back to Ireland as soon as I can make the necessary arrangements.

MITCHELL: This is pretty unexpected.

BISHOP: Well, I had been thinking it over for some time and I mentioned it to the Apostolic Delegate, who thought it was a good idea. Or he mentioned it to me, I forget which. But it was my own decision, to all intents and purposes. The diocese needs a younger man at the top, especially now in these troubled times, a younger man.

MITCHELL: Has the new man been appointed?

BISHOP: It hasn't been easy finding a successor. I was asked for my recommendation, of course, and I knew it would carry a good deal of weight. To be frank, I would have thought that you had many of the necessary qualities, but then one has to take account of the opinions of others. In particular, I was thinking about your drink problem—

MITCHELL: I wouldn't say I had a drink problem.

BISHOP: I know that, I know that, but people talk all the same, don't they? And there's no smoke without a fire. There was the time you insulted that Monsignor from Propaganda and there was the speech you made at Mother Gertrude's Golden Jubilee dinner. Some of the references to the early history of Uzala were a bit inappropriate to the occasion. Granted, it was a trivial incident. It could have happened to a b— it could have happened to anyone. But people talk. And then there is this business of Africanization. Rome is pushing very hard for more African bishops, prematurely in my

[15]

view, but pushing very hard, and unless you have an outstanding white man you can recommend, it's very hard to resist that kind of pressure. I don't mind telling you I feel quite exhausted by the whole business now that it's over.

MITCHELL: Who is the new bishop? Or am I allowed to ask?

BISHOP: I thought you might have gussed by now. It's Zachary.

MITCHEL.: Zachary? Our Zachary?

BISHOP: He was really the only possible choice under the circumstances. And in many ways he's quite suitable. He's been educated abroad, he speaks good English, he's quite presentable.

MITCHELL: Oh yes, you could take him anywhere, he eats with a knife and fork, he's clean about the house. He'd make a good head altar-boy. But a bishop? He will be a total and unrelieved disaster. Have you told him?

BISHOP: That he's going to be a disaster?

MITCHELL: That he's going to be bishop.

BISHOP: Yes, just now. I had to make the formal announcement and ask for his consent.

MITCHELL: That didn't take long.

BISHOP: No. I may be old-fashioned, but I preferred the traditional display of reluctance. I remember when I was appointed—I was in Dublin at the time—I got this urgent message that the Nuncio wanted to see me. Well, it wasn't too hard to guess what he wanted to see me about and I was well briefed by the lads before I went up to the Park. So when he popped the question, I said how overwhelmed I was and unworthy and all that and would he mind if I retired to his private oratory to spend a few minutes in prayer before I gave him my answer. He said "But of course, my dear Father" and obviously felt pleased that I was making the appropriate response under the circumstances.

MITCHELL: And did you?

BISHOP: Did I what?

MITCHELL: Spend a few minutes in prayer?

BISHOP: Yes, indeed I did. In fact, I finished off my office for for the day because I knew the lads were planning a bit of a celebration when I got back. Yes. It may sound cynical, but even if one has one's mind made up, there is a certain

[16]

decorum that should be observed on these occasions, don't you think? I mean, what would you do in a case like that?

MITCHELL: Even by your standards, My Lord, that is a remarkably tactless question.

BISHOP: I'm sorrry. I must be getting old.

MITCHELL: It doesn't matter.

BISHOP: I think I'd better be going. I promised to call at the convent.

MITCHELL: You'll be coming back for chop?

BISHOP: No, I won't, if you don't mind. The way things are, I'd like to get home before it's dark.

MITCHELL: Safe journey, then.

BISHOP: Thanks. Look after yourself, Father Joe. [*No answer.*] God bless.

[*The bishop goes. Mitchell pours himself a drink and drinks it quickly. Then he pours another and sits on the verandah with the glass in his hand. Cyprian comes in softly. The light begins to fade.*]

CYPRIAN: Father. [*No answer. He speaks louder.*] Father.

MITCHELL: Yes? Cyprian?

CYPRIAN: How many will there be for chop, Father?

MATCHELL: Just thrcc. The bishop is not staying.

CYPRIAN: Yes, Father. [*He hesitates.*] Father.

MITCHELL: Yes?

CYPRIAN: May I talk to you, Father?

MITCHELL: Yes. Sit down. [*Cyprian sits on step of verandah.*] What is it?

CYPRIAN: Is there really going to be a war, Father?

MITCHELL: I don't know, Cyprian. I think there will be.

CYPRIAN: I'm afraid of being killed.

MITCHELL: So am I. So are we all.

CYPRIAN: Will I have to fight, Father?

MITCHELL: I don't know that, either. If there is a war and it goes on for a long time, everyone may have to fight.

CYPRIAN: Will you have to fight, Father?

MITCHELL: Well no, I'm a foreigner.

CYPRIAN: Will Father Zachary have to fight?

MITCHELL: No, he won't.

CYPRIAN: Why not, Father?

[17]

MITCHELL: Because he's a priest and priests aren't expected to fight.

CYPRIAN: Father—

MITCHELL: Yes—

CYPRIAN: I want to be a priest, too.

MITCHELL: Wait now, you can't be a priest just to avoid fighting. You have to have a vocation, you have to be called by God.

CYPRIAN: It's not just to avoid fighting. I want to be a priest anyhow. That's what I want to talk to you about.

MITCHELL: Why do you want to be a priest?

CYPRIAN: I don't know, Father. I just think it's what I want to be.

MITCHELL: That's not a very good reason, is it?

CYPRIAN: Why did you become a priest, Father?

MITCHELL: Me? It's so long ago I hardly remember. I probably didn't even know at the time.

CYPRIAN: If there is a war, there will be many people killed and many people injured. After the war there will be women without men and children without parents. There will be sorrow and loss. There will be need for priests.

MITCHELL: Why don't you talk to Father Zachary about this?

CYPRIAN: I'd rather talk to you, Father.

MITCHELL: I'm not terribly good at this sort of thing. You're sure you wouldn't like to be a teacher or a bank maanger or a sanitary inspector or something?

CYPRIAN: No, Father.

MITCHELL: There are a whole lot of pious things that are supposed to be said on an occasion like this but I'm damned if I'm going to say them. All the same, I think you might be serious about this and I want to be serious about it too. How old were you when you left school?

CYPRIAN: Sixteen, Father.

MITCHELL: And how old are you now?

CYPRIAN: Eighteen.

MITCHELL: You would have to go to the seminary for a lot more study—

CYPRIAN: I know, Father.

MITCHELL: And if there is a war, the seminary will probably be closed down. You may have to wait a long time.

[18]

CYPRIAN: I can wait. It is my aim and I will follow it relentlessly.

MITCHELL: You do that, Cyprian. And say your prayers relentlessly too, because we're all going to need them. We'll talk about this again. I'm a bit tired now.

CYPRIAN: Yes, Father. Will I switch on the light, Father?

MITCHELL: No, leave it for the moment.

[*Cyprian goes back to kitchen. During preceding scene dusk has fallen and the living room has become quite dark. Mitchell sits a while in thought, sipping at his glass. A light comes on over the table and the bishop is seen sitting behind it, dressed in a plain black soutane.*]

BISHOP: Come in. [*Mitchell starts. Louder.*] Come in. [*Mitchell rises and walks over to the desk.*] Ah, yes. Mitchell. Sit down, my boy, sit down. And what can I do for you?

MITCHELL: You sent for me, Father.

BISHOP: So I did, so I did. Yes, indeed. Cigarette?

MITCHELL: No, thank you, Father.

BISHOP: Go on, it's all right, I want you to make yourself at home.

MITCHELL: I don't smoke, Father.

BISHOP: You're very wise. And you don't drink either.

MITCHELL: No, Father.

BISHOP: And never will, I hope. Now let me see. You will be leaving school next summer.

MITCHELL: Yes, Father.

BISHOP: And you're seventeen, eighteen?

MITCHELL: Eighteen next birthday.

BISHOP: A wonderful age, Mitchell, a wonderful age. You don't mind if I call you John? [*No answer.*] Your name is John, isn't it?

MITCHELL: Joe.

BISHOP: I meant Joe. Yes, Joe, a wonderful age. Your life stretches before you like a smiling landscape, a thousand paths, an infinity of opportunities. But only one of those paths is the right one for you, the one divinely appointed for you to walk on. It's a solemn thought, it's a solemn thought, Mitchell—John—Joe.

MITCHELL: Yes, Father.

BISHOP: I want you to remember that I am here to help you.

[19]

Don't look on me as your Dean but as your friend who wants to assist you at this crossroads of your life. There's no one so strong but needs some help, no one so weak but has some help to give. That's true, isn't it, Michael?

MITCHELL: Yes, Father.

BISHOP: I have to watch your progress because it's part of my job and I must say you impress me as a boy of many good qualities. You may be a bit headstrong at times—you don't mind me saying this?—

MITCHELL: No, Father.

BISHOP: But it's a small point. You get on well with the other boys, you attend to your religious duties, you work well at your studies. What is your favourite subject?

MITCHELL: Er—

BISHOP: Do you like Latin?

MITCHELL: Yes, Father.

BISHOP: As indeed you should. The language of Cicero, the language of Augustine, the language of Aquinas. The language which gives most perfect expression to rhetoric and to philosophy and to prayer. Latin brings us back to the roots of our civilization and of our religion. A dead language, but more alive than any living language. The words that I speak as a priest each morning at Mass, those selfsame words echo right back along the centuries, back to Constantine, back to Irenaeus, back almost to the time of the Apostles. That is why I have always loved Latin.

MITCHELL: I think I prefer chemistry.

BISHOP [*Suspecting insolence but not sure*]: What do you intend to do when you leave school?

MITCHELL: I don't know, Father.

BISHOP: You don't know?

MITCHELL: I haven't made up my mind.

BISHOP: Have you no idea?

MITCHELL: I was thinking of science, Father.

BISHOP: Any particular branch of science?

MITCHELL: Nothing very definite.

BISHOP: It's a coming profession. You could do very well for yourself, make a lot of money, if that's what you think your life is for. But I don't think that's what your life is for,

[20]

and unless I'm very much mistaken, you don't either. Do you?

MITCHELL: I suppose not, Father.

BISHOP: What do you think your life is for?

MITCHELL [*Embarrassed*]: To do good, I suppose.

BISHOP: What kind of good?

MITCHELL: Just good.

BISHOP: Could we be more precise? Could we say to save the souls of others and to save your own?

MITCHELL: Yes, Father.

BISHOP: And would you say that you could do that by becoming a priest?

MITCHELL: I suppose so.

BISHOP: Have you ever thought of becoming a priest?

MITCHELL: No, Father.

BISHOP: Never given it a moment's consideration?

MITCHELL: No, Father.

BISHOP: In this school no attempt is made to force any boy's conscience. At the same time, it is our duty to propose the ideal of the priesthood to our students and I don't think that we neglect that duty. The subject is mentioned in class, in chapel, in private conversation. Every year at the annual retreat, you are invited to reflect and to pray about this matter. And yet you sit there and tell me that the thought of the priesthood never even entered your mind?

MITCHELL: Well, it entered my mind but I just didn't think it was for me.

BISHOP: I think perhaps it is for you. I think you have an idealism, a generosity of spirit, that cannot be satisfied by anything less than a complete giving to God. I think if you were to join our Congregation, you could do great work for him on the missions. And I am not alone in that opinion. I have spoken to Father Delaney about you. He tells me that you and he have discussed this on several occasions.

MITCHELL: Anything I said to Father Delaney was in confidence. He had no right to break that confidence to anyone.

BISHOP: There is no need to be impertinent, Mitchell. Father Delaney was only trying to help. Wanting to be a priest is not something to be ashamed of. Why try to hide it from me?

MITCHELL: It's just that I haven't really made up my mind.

[21]

BISHOP: My job is to help you make up your mind. I said I wanted you to look on me as a friend. I meant that. I want you to feel free to come in here and talk about the things that really matter, to open your heart and mind to me. You'll do that, won't you, Mitchell?

MITCHELL: Yes, Father.

BISHOP: I wonder, I wonder. You know—er—Joe—you know we're on the same side, you and I, we're on the same side. In this enclosed petty world of school it is easy to draw rigid lines, to label people as friends or enemies. It's easy and it's wrong and it's wasteful. There is a battle-line drawn somewhere between good and evil but it doesn't run through our little community. I'm not sure where it runs. The older I get, the further away it seems. But, be that as it may, you and I are on the same side, and as you grow older you'll see it more clearly. Perhaps some time in the future we will be working together in some African country we've never even heard of, working together as servants of the same Master, the Master who said: "I will not call you servants but friends." Friendship isn't something that can be forced on anyone. He doesn't force it on us. I don't force it on you. It must take its course. You don't have to accept it right away. But you don't have to reject it either, do you? Try to treat me as a human being, just as I try to treat you as a human being. You will try, won't you?

MITCHELL: Yes, Father.

BISHOP: Right. I look forward to having another little chat with you soon. I'll see you at Rugby practice on Thursday afternoon. By the way I didn't see you last Thursday afternoon. Were you sick?

MITCHELL: Actually, I don't like Rugby. In fact I hate it.

BISHOP: Once again, Mitchell, there's no need to be impertinent. We all have to do things we don't like. That will be all, Mitchell. [*He rises and goes out.*]

MITCHELL: Yes, Father, anything you say. You nearly got through my defences that time, Father. [*He rises and returns to the verandah.*] But there's nothing like a winter of dark evenings on a freezing Rugby pitch to put things into perspective. It's surprising how clear your thoughts on friend-

[22]

ship become when your socks are full of water and your mouth is full of mud. Did you ever take a look at yourself, Maurice FitzMaurice, clumping around in people's lives, did you ever notice the blood on your hobnailed boots? The Maurice Fitz-Maurice instant solve-your-problem service. Incorporating dial-a-message and rent-a-friend. Pardon me, Mister, but that's my soul you're standing on. [*He pauses, then takes up his breviary and opens it, still standing.*] Let us pray for our friends and for our enemies, if we have any. [*He crosses himself.*] In nomine Patris et Filii et Spiritus Sancti. Amen. [*Still reading his breviary he moves off in the direction of the bedrooms. As he leaves the living room he switches off the light. The stage is now in complete darkness.*]

The lights come up again. It is mid-morning, one year later. There is little change except that the room is a little shabbier. The photograph of the bishop has been replaced by a similar one of his successor.

Sister Eileen comes up on to the verandah from the direction of the convent. She is in her late twenties and is dressed in a neat modern style habit.

EILEEN: Hello, anybody in? [*Mitchell comes out, wearing his white soutane.*] Good morning, Father.

MITCHELL: Sister Eileen, you are the light of my life.

EILEEN: Happy birthday!

MITCHELL: Thank you. [*Thinks.*] I'm fifty today?

EILEEN: Are you?

MITCHELL: Well, whose birthday is it?

EILEEN: Don't you know?

MITCHELL: Yours? You're fifty today? Twenty-one?

EILEEN: Try again.

MITCHELL: Mother Gertrude. She's a hundred and thirty-eight.

EILEEN: You're impossible. Don't you know that the Republic of Biafra is one year old today? This is Independence Day.

MITCHELL: So it is, so it is. I'm sure this calls for a brief burst of martial music by way of celebration.

EILEEN: If you think you've anything to celebrate. Personally, I think we might have been better off if the Federals had

[23]

taken over the place in the first few weeks.

MITCHELL: And slaughtered all the people?

EILEEN: They're dying of hunger anyway so what's the difference?

MITCHELL: The difference is that Father Tony has just got back from the conference in Orlu and things are defintely looking up. That's why I asked you over. Is Gertrude coming too?

EILEEN: No. And she made me promise to be back in half an hour. We've had five more children in the last twenty-four hours.

MITCHELL: Kwashi-orkor?

EILEEN: Yes. Arms and legs like matchsticks and tummies all swelled out. They're celebrating Independence Day on Complan—at least, four of them are.

MITCHELL: And the fifth?

EILEEN: He's celebrating Independence Day in Heaven.

MITCHELL: It gets you down sometimes?

EILEEN: You do your best, that's all you can do. It's not easy when you never have enough of anything. We now have exactly one hypodermic syringe left. And I succeeded in breaking our last thermometer yesterday. We can't even take anyone's temperature any more.

MITCHELL: How did you enjoy that tin of ham I sent you over?

EILEEN: I—er—it was very good ham.

MITCHELL: It wasn't good ham. It was stringy and salty. But that wasn't the question. I asked you how you enjoyed it.

EILEEN: Well, you know how it is.

MITCHELL: Yes, I know how it is. By incredible exertions I get you the only tin of meat in the whole of Biafra and you then give it to the first fellow that comes along and spins you a hard-luck story. Was he a good actor?

EILEEN: It was a family of five and they were pretty good actors. Their legs were covered with ulcers and you could count their ribs.

MITCHELL: You win. You always win. It's no use arguing with nuns. I don't know why I even try. I know you're going to kill yourself but what does it matter to you? You'll die like Robert Emmet with a smile upon your lips.

[*Father O'Brien enters, dressed in shirt and shorts, from inside the house.*]

[24]

O'BRIEN: Hello, Sister dear.

EILEEN: Hello, Father. How did the trip go?

O'BRIEN: Great, just great. Things are really looking up. Did Father Joe tell you?

EILEEN: Not yet.

O'BRIEN: Well, the first thing is, we are now going to win the war. There has been a definite stabilization all along the front line.

MITCHELL: By stabilization you mean stalemate?

O'BRIEN: Stalemate is all we need. We're not trying to attack, we're just trying to survive.

MITCHELL: When you say "We are going to win the war," I take it you mean "They are going to win the war"?

O'BRIEN: They? The Federals?

MITCHELL: They. The Biafrans.

O'BRIEN: I don't get it.

MITCHELL: It's not our war. It's their war, and don't you forget it. It's not a missionary's job to get mixed up in politics.

O'BRIEN: This isn't politics, it's people's lives. But maybe missionaries aren't supposed to get themselves mixed up with that either?

MITCHELL: We are foreigners in a foreign country. This war isn't going to last forever. Maybe we would like to see the Ibos winning but there's a fifty-fifty chance they'll lose. And what'll happen to us then?

O'BRIEN: Well, what will happen to us?

MITCHELL: That depends on what we do now. If we let ourselves become identified with the Biafran side, then we'll be thrown out, and fifty years of missionary work will have gone for nothing.

O'BRIEN: So what do we do? Do we let ten million people die of starvation while we are poncing around in our political chastity belts?

MITCHELL: We do our job, that's what we do. We baptize, we preach the word, we feed the hungry, we clothe the naked, we care for the sick. But we try not to talk or even to think as if the Biafrans were us and the Nigerians were them.

EILEEN: Excuse me, Fathers, but do you think we could get down to business? If I'm not back in the convent in a few minutes, I'll be walled up alive or something.

O'BRIEN: Right. Situation is this. The Churches have managed to get a few beat-up old Constellations on to Sao Tomé and they're going to run a regular airlift into Biafra every night. They reckon they can get in a hundred tons a night for starters—food, medicine, petrol, spare parts, anything that's needed to keep us going apart from military supplies.

EILEEN: It sounds fine but can they really do it?

O'BRIEN: They are doing it. The airlift has been working now for nearly a week. The warehouse at Orlu is bulging with stuff. All we have to do is make out a detailed list of what we need and send a lorry every second day to collect it.

MITCHELL: Is there any lorry around in working order?

EILEEN: There's Innocent Mapwepwe's.

MITCHELL: "In God We Trust"?

EILEEN: That's the one.

O'BRIEN: In God we trust?

MITCHELL: He's got "In God We Trust" written over the driver's cab. It was cheaper than getting a new set of brake linings . . .

EILEEN: I think it's in some kind of working order.

MITCHELL: We should be able to get it started all right. Stopping it is another question but that won't arise until later.

EILEEN: You don't know what it's been like trying to carry on the clinic with never enough of anything. You can't even give a patient an aspirin without worrying whether there'll be another patient tomorrow that'll need it more. I think you're wonderful, I really do.

O'BRIEN: Woman, your flattery means nothing to me. It runs off me like water off a duck's back.

MITCHELL: But the duck loves it.

O'BRIEN: Anyhow, I had nothing to do with it. All I'm doing is passing on the good news.

MITCHELL: But it has always been customary to praise and reward the bearer of good news. I propose a little celebration. I told you a lie a few minutes ago, Sister. I said I had given you the last tin of meat in Biafra. It wasn't. It was only the second last tin. We shall have the last this very day for lunch and you, Sister, shall eat your share. I'll go now and get it from its secret hiding-place.

[26]

EILEEN: No, really, I can't stay. Mother wouldn't hear of it.

MITCHELL: One word from Mother and she'll get a two-pound tin of bully beef right between the eyes. You do what you're told, girl. I'm giving the orders round here today. [*He goes out.*]

O'BRIEN: So.

EILEEN: So.

O'BRIEN: How are things since? Any air-raids?

EILEEN: Nothing much. They dropped a bomb in the bush near Mbutu and they machine-gunned an old woman. That was all.

O'BRIEN: I wish you wouldn't wear that white. It makes you too conspicuous.

EILEEN: You don't expect me to wear black in this climate?

O'BRIEN: No, but something coloured. A bit of camouflage. Something that wouldn't be noticed from the air.

EILEEN: And what do you think Reverend Mother would say if I appeared out in technicolour?

O'BRIEN: Yes, what would she say? That's what's important, isn't it? Not whether you live or die. Your whole life is dominated by that crazy old bag.

EILEEN: Oh, she's not all that bad. It's just that it's hard to change your ideas at that age.

O'BRIEN: Because she was kicked around by her Reverend Mother when she was young, she thinks she has to do the same to you. She has you scared out of your wits.

EILEEN: Actually, we get on very well. All the same, I don't think I ought to stay for lunch. It isn't customary.

O'BRIEN: It isn't customary to have meat but we're having it today. How long is it since you've had any?

EILEEN: You're trying to lead me into temptation.

O'BRIEN: It's a temptation recommended by the best theologians. Father Faber says there are three classes of men given to gluttony: the rich by way of ostentation, the studious by way of relaxation, the clergy by way of compensation.

EILEEN: I was always told that gluttony was a sin.

O'BRIEN: If you can commit a sin on the amount you get today, good luck to you. But anyhow, when we get the ground transport organized, there should be a regular supply of meat for all the missions. There are a few bugs but I'll be able to work on them.

EILEEN: You're really rather enjoying this, aren't you?

O'BRIEN: Well, it's a challenge. I suppose I am enjoying it in a way. You aren't?

EILEEN: No.

O'BRIEN: Not at all?

EILEEN: Not at all.

O'BRIEN: Do you not even feel a bit of pride at being in at the birth of a nation and sharing the glory as well as the pain? Do you not get the feeling we're all in this together, it's us against them?

EILEEN: Father Joe wouldn't agree with you.

O'BRIEN: If he thinks any of us can be neutral in this war, he's quite wrong. Just by bringing in food we're taking sides, we're making it possible for Biafra to carry on. The people are quite clear that we're on their side. That drive back from Orlu this morning—it was just fantastic. I had a Caritas sticker on the windscreen of the car and it was like a presidential banner. All along the side of the road people stood and cheered as I was passing by. Kids shouted "Caritas," men waved, soldiers got off their bicycles and saluted. At the road-blocks I was waved through. And you know that broken-down old eating-house opposite Jimmy Prendergast's church—it used to be called the Manhattan United Nations Restaurant?

EILEEN: I remember it.

O'BRIEN: It's been renamed in honour of the birthplace of the parish priest and it's now called the Lisdoonvarna Imperial Ice-Cream Parlour. God, there'll be great match-making there when they have the hay in.

EILEEN: There will be if there's anyone left alive.

O'BRIEN: As I said before, we're going to win this war. And even if a lot of us have to suffer, it's suffering that binds us together. Because the missionaries are staying on and sharing that suffering we've become part of the people like we never were before. Sooner or later, some of us will be injured or even killed and it will be very sad and all that; but it will mean that we have become part of Biafra's history, part of the one minute's silence on Biafra's Armistice Day.

EILEEN: Well, have it your own way. But personally I think I can do more good tying bandages than bleeding all over the pages of the history books.

O'BRIEN: You're right. I'm too full of these wild romantic ideas. I'm going to be very pratical from now on. I'm going to stop making patriotic speeches and take up bookkeeping. And I'm going to get Cyprian to give me a good military-style hair-cut.

EILEEN: Oh, don't. I like your hair the way it is. [*She pauses in embarrassment.*] I'm sorry, I didn't mean it that way. [*Pauses again.*] Do you think it's very hot today?

O'BRIEN: Yes. It's hot all the time. We're in Africa. Would you like something to drink?

EILEEN: Have you any orange-juice?

O'BRIEN: It's about the only thing we have, apart from palm-wine. [*He pours two drinks from the fridge.*]

EILEEN: What's keeping Father Joe?

O'BRIEN: He's probably checking his supplies. Actually, he has quite a store in the sacristy, behind the vestment press. I found it by accident a couple of weeks ago.

EILEEN: What's he got there? Tins?

O'BRIEN: More in the way of bottles, I'd say. But that's his business, not mine.

EILEEN: I feel sorry for him. He would have made a lovely bishop.

O'BRIEN: You feel sorry for everyone.

EILEEN: I know. I can't help it. He reminds me a bit of our bishop back home. I knew him well. He was my mother's uncle.

O'BRIEN: I didn't know that.

EILEEN: For the last ten years of his life he was never what you could call really sober. But he was a lovely man. You should have seen the crowds at his funeral. I cried my eyes out.

O'BRIEN: There are fifty thousand alcoholics in Ireland and fifty thousand nicer men you never met in all your life. Your good health, sister dear.

[*They clink glasses and drink, just in time to be seen by Mother Gertrude as she enters. She is in her seventies and wears an old-fashioned white habit.*]

GERTRUDE: Sister Eileen.

O'BRIEN: Oh, hello, Mother.

GERTRUDE: Good morning, Father. I hope I am not interrupting your meeting.

O'BRIEN: No, the meeting is more or less over.

GERTRUDE: Yes, I thought it was when I saw Father Mitchell going over to the church.

O'BRIEN: Would you like to join us in a genteel booze-up?

GERTRUDE: Thank you, Father, but we are very busy in the clinic, as I'm sure Sister Eileen has told you. I was expecting her back as soon as the meeting was finished.

O'BRIEN: Actually, she's staying on here for a spot of lunch with us. You'd be very welcome too, if you like. Father Joe has a whole tinned ox ready for the roasting.

GERTRUDE: I'm sorry but it won't be possible for either of us. Sister Eileen is very grateful for the invitation but she has to go at once.

O'BRIEN [*Getting angry*]: Perhaps Sister Eileen is capable of making up her own mind and expressing her own opinion?

EILEEN: Excuse me, Father, but I think I'd better go.
[*She goes out quickly. On the verandah she meets Mitchell returning with the tin of meat but brushes past him without a word.*]

O'BRIEN: What exactly do you think you have achieved by that, apart from feeding your own megalomania?

GERTRUDE: With all respect, Father, I think you placed Sister Eileen in a false position. I allowed her to come over to represent the sisters at a meeting with the two priests, not a tete-a-tete with one of them.

O'BRIEN: What the hell do you mean by a tete-a-tete?

GERTRUDE: I just mean a tete-a-tete.

O'BRIEN: I see. Well, I'm going after Sister Eileen and I'm going to tell her what I'm too polite to tell you, that her Reverend Mother is a filthy-minded old faggot!
[*He goes out after Eileen. Gertrude turns to Mitchell who has entered the room during the preceding exchange.*]

GERTRUDE: That's nice language, Father. Did you hear what he called me?

[30]

MITCHELL: Yes, he called you a filthy-minded old faggot. However he was speaking on the spur of the moment. I'm sure if he'd had time to think, he could have expressed himself more suitably.

GERTRUDE: I think you should speak to him about it.

MITCHELL: I'm sure I should if only I knew what to say. I suppose I could tell him he spoke to you very rudely but I imagine he would answer that you spoke to him very rudely.

GERTRUDE: I never even raised my voice to him.

MITCHELL: No, you just arrived on the scene like a one-woman Catholic Rescue and Protection Society and snatched Sister Eileen from a fate worse than death.

GERTRUDE: I'm sorry to see you taking his side.

MITCHELL: I'm not taking his side, I'm just telling you the way he looks at it. He may be over-sensitive but you must remember that he is going through a period of great strain. So is she.

GERTRUDE: Father, that is something that I am not likely to forget. I pray for them constantly, both of them, that God will give them the strength they need to carry their daily burden. They are young and they are living in troubled times, and there is the danger that they might look for strength and consolation apart from God. I have lived long enough in this world to know that what is natural isn't always what is good. I would be failing in my duty if I didn't point this out to them and so, if you don't mind me saying so, would you.

MITCHELL: I'm afraid I've grown accustomed to being a failure.

GERTRUDE: I won't take up any more of your time, Father.

MITCHELL: Wait a moment. [*He listens.*] I'm not sure that I like the sound of that too much.

GERTRUDE: What is it?

MITCHELL: I'm not sure.

[*Cyprian runs in.*]

CYPRIAN: Father, it is an enemy plane. It is a mig, it is coming this way. Keep away from the windows. [*He takes charge.*] You must take cover.

MITCHELL: Where?

CYPRIAN: Under the table. Lie face down with your hands over the back of your neck. That is what it says in the handbook.

GERTRUDE: I'm not getting under that table.

[31]

CYPRIAN: Yes, yes, hurry please. You must obey the regulations scrupulously.

[*He succeeds in getting the three of them under the table. The plane comes close and there is the sound of a number of bursts of machine-gun fire. Plaster falls from the ceiling, a window breaks. Then the noise dies away gradually. Cyprian rises.*]

CYPRIAN: You can get up now. Many civilian lives would be saved if persons took proper precautions.

[*He and Mitchell help Gertrude to her feet.*]

MITCHELL: Are you all right, Mother? Oh, my back! I'd rather be shot any day. [*He starts to brush his clothes with his hand.*] [*O'Brien comes up on the verandah and into the house. He is carrying Eileen in his arms. She is motionless and her white habit is soaked in blood. Gertrude sees them first.*]

GERTRUDE: Jesus, Mary and Joseph!

[*O'Brien lays her down on a bench in the room and then stands back.*]

MITCHELL: What happened?

O'RBIEN: She was shot. Machine-gunned. By the plane. I shouted to her to get down but she didn't seem to hear.

[*Gertrude kneels beside her and says the Act of Contrition into her ear.*]

GERTRUDE: O my God, I am heartily sorry for having offended Thee, and I detest my sins above every other evil because they displease Thee, my God, who for Thy infinite goodness art so deserving of all my love; and I firmly resolve by Thy holy grace never more to offend Thee and to amend my life.

[*While she is praying, Mitchell administers the last rites. He takes a purple stole from his pocket and puts it around his neck, and makes the sign of the cross over her.*]

MITCHELL: Ego te absolvo a peccatis tuis, in nomine Patris et Filii et Spiritus Sancti. Amen. [*He then takes the oil of anointing from a drawer and signs her forehead with oil.*] Per istam sanctam unctionem et suam piissiman misericordiam indulgeat tibi Dominus quidquid deliquisti. Amen.

O'BRIEN: Do something. Can we get a doctor? Can we get her to a proper hospital somewhere?

MITCHELL: Tony. Tony, she's dead.

O'BRIEN: Oh my God. Why did it have to be her? She was the

[32]

best of the lot of us.

[*Gertrude gets a white sheet from somewhere.*]

GERTRUDE: She lived for the people of Uzala and she died for them. She wouldn't have wanted it any other way.

O'BRIEN: She didn't want to die.

GERTRUDE [*Covering Eileen with sheet*]: She looks quite peaceful. There's almost a smile on her lips.

MITCHELL: Yes. [*He moves away.*]

GERTRUDE [*Kneeling*]: Eternal rest grant unto her, O Lord.

CYPRIAN [*Kneeling*]: And let perpetual light shine upon her.

GERTRUDE: May she rest in peace.

CYPRIAN: Amen.

GERTRUDE: May her soul and the souls of all the faithful departed through the mercy of God rest in peace.

CYPRIAN: Amen.

MITCHELL: Yes. A smile upon her lips. Just like Robert Emmet.

END OF ACT ONE.

ACT TWO

The scene is the same as Act One but a further year and a half have passed. The house has become very dilapidated and there are still some traces of the air attack visible. The living room is untidy, with cardboard boxes piled in one corner and a couple of sacks of meal in another. It is night.

Mitchell is seated at the table, having just finished his evening meal.

MITCHELL: Cyprian!

CYPRIAN [*Entering*]: Yes, Father.

MITCHELL: You can clear away the table. I don't think Father O'Brien will be here for chop.

CYPRIAN: Yes, Father. [*Clears away table.*] Father, may I speak to you? [*He is shifty and uneasy.*]

MITCHELL: Of course.

CYPRIAN: I must go away at once. I must go to see my father. He is very sick.

MITCHELL: I'm sorry to hear that. What is wrong with him?

CYPRIAN: I do not know, Father. He is very sick.

MITCHELL: Where is he now?

CYPRIAN: I do not know, Father.

MITCHELL: Then how are you going to see him?

CYPRIAN: I will find him. I will see him, wherever he is.

MITCHELL [*Growing suspicious*]: How do you know he's sick?

CYPRIAN: I got a message, Father.

MITCHELL: From whom?

CYPRIAN: From a man.

MITCHELL: What man?

CYPRIAN: I do not know his name.

MITCHELL: Cyprian, we've known each other for a good while. We've been through more than two years of war together. There is no reason why you should stand there and tell me lies.

CYPRIAN: I am not telling lies, Father. It is necessary for me to go.

MITCHELL: It is necessary for you to stay. You were exempted from the army because you were helping in the clinic. You can't just disappear like that.

CYPRIAN: Yes, Father, I must go.

MITCHELL: Cyprian, there are twenty patients in the clinic, which was only built as a treatment centre for out-patients. There is also a school which has been turned into a hospital for kwashi-orkor children—between fifty and sixty of them, depending on how many have died in the last six hours. You are the only man left to do the heavy work for the sisters, to carry the sick people, to cut wood for the kitchen. If you leave, who is going to do it? They are your people, Cyprian, and it's you they need to help them.

CYPRIAN: I do help them, Father. I work very hard. I even went in the plane with the children to Sao Tomé, and I was very frightened.

MITCHELL: You went in the plane with the children to Sao Tomé and what did you do when you got there?

CYPRIAN: I looked after them.

MITCHELL: You were supposed to look after them and settle them in the refugees camp. But I was told that you went into the town instead and bought things in the shops.

[34]

CYPRIAN: No, Father, it's not true.

MITCHELL: And I was told that you spent some of the children's money.

CYPRIAN: No, Father, it's not true.

MITCHELL: That's a nice belt you're wearing, I never saw that before. It's new, isn't it? Where did you get it? [*No answer.*] Where did you get it, Cyprian?

CYPRIAN [*Softly*]: I bought it in Sao Tomé

MITCHELL: I see.

CYPRIAN: I hear the car, Father. I must go.

MITCHELL: Go where?

CYPRIAN: I will help Father O'Brien to bring in his things.

MITCHELL: If Father O'Brien wants help, he will call you. Just stay where you are.

[*O'Brien comes in with a box of groceries. He is without his glasses.*]

O'BRIEN: Greetings from Uli and one week's supply of fleshpots. I'm afraid it's tinned ham again.

MITCHELL: Have you eaten?

O'BRIEN: Yes, I called in to Jimmy Prendergast. His cook has a new recipe for tinned ham.

O'BRIEN: He boils it in palm wine.

MITCHELL: What does it taste like?

O'BRIEN: Tinned ham. But the gravy is terrific.

MITCHELL: Would you like Cyprian to get you a cup of coffee?

O'BRIEN: O.K.

CYPRIAN: I have no coffee, Father.

O'BRIEN: There's some in the box.

CYPRIAN: Thank you, Father. [*He goes out with the box.*]

MITCHELL: Well, what's the news from the outside world? Any letters from home?

O'BRIEN: Nothing this time. There's a note from Patsy Finnegan in Orlu inviting you to a St. Brigid's night party. [*Hands over letter.*]

MITCHELL: St. Brigid's night? It always used to St. Patrick's night. [*He starts to read letter, which was in sealed envelope.*]

O'BRIEN: He says he's not sure if there'll be any Biafra left by St. Patrick's night.

MITCHELL: He always was a pessimist. [*Reads letter.*] He sug-

[35]

gests that when I am coming to the party I could bring along the bottle of whiskey, if there is any of it left.

O'RBIEN [*Startled*]: The bottle of whiskey?

MITCHELL: That's right. The bottle of whiskey from my mother which he gave you this morning to deliver.

O'BRIEN: Oh yes.

MITCHELL: You remember it?

O'BRIEN: Yes.

MITCHELL: Well?

O'BRIEN: Well?

MITCHELL: Well, have you got it or did you drink it on the way?

O'RBIEN: No.

MITCHELL: No, you haven't got it, or no, you didn't drink it on the way?

O'BRIEN: The truth of the matter is, I lost it.

MITCHELL: I see. Forgive me if I seem inquisitorial, but further down here I see a jocular reference to other bottles of a similar nature which were also given to you for delivery. None of them have ever arrived here, to my knowledge. Did you lose them also?

O'BRIEN: Yes, I did.

MITCHELL: All of them?

O'BRIEN: Yes.

MITCHELL: That's what I admire about you. You're so thorough.

O'BRIEN: The fact is, I lost them deliberately.

MITCHELL: You can't lose a thing deliberately.

O'BRIEN: I didn't exactly lose them. It was more by way of selling them.

MITCHELL: You sold them?

O'BRIEN: I sold them in the market. There's quite a demand for whiskey at the moment.

MITCHELL: The next market isn't for three days. You hardly had time to sell the latest bottle, did you?

O'BRIEN: No.

MITCHELL: Where is it?

O'BRIEN: In the car.

MITCHELL: Would you mind getting it, please?

[*Tony goes out. Mitchell gets a glass from the sideboard. Tony returns with the bottle.*]

MITCHELL: Thank you. [*He opens bottle and pours a drink.*] I'm sorry to deprieve you of what has no doubt become a regular source of income, but these little gifts have a sentimental value for me. Cheers! [*He drinks.*]

O'BRIEN: I didn't sell them for myself. I sold them to buy yams for the kids.

MITCHELL: If that's meant to be an explanation, it's not a very adequate one.

O'BRIEN: I thought the yams were good for the kids. And I thought the whiskey was bad for you. That's all. Now hit me if you want to.

MITCHELL: Hit you? Raise my impious hand against you and be struck dead upon the spot?

O'BRIEN: Oh, come off it.

MITCHELL: I can recognize moral superiority when I see it. And the fact that my immediate impulse is to shove your teeth down your sanctimonious throat is just another proof of my degeneracy.

O'BRIEN [*Angered*]: I'm not saying I'm perfect but at least I try to face up to myself. I don't drink myself stupid every time a problem comes along.

MITCHELL: You don't have to drink yourself stupid. Nature has already taken care of that.

O'BRIEN: I know I'm not a match for you in the line of sparkling dialogue so I won't try. All I'll say is this. I like you and I admire you and it makes me very sad to see you destroying yourself. If you want to dig your own grave, I can't stop you. But I'm not going to hand you the shovel.

MITCHELL [*More friendly*]: Would you like some?

O'BRIEN: No.

MITCHELL [*Pours another glass*]: You might as well. It means there will be less for me, which is a good thing. Anyhow, you need it. You're shaking all over.

O'BRIEN [*Takes glass*]: Thanks. [*Drinks.*]

MITCHELL: You have your problems too, haven't you?

O'BRIEN: Yes.

MITCHELL: Would you like to tell me? Some of them anyhow?

O'BRIEN: I don't know how much longer I can carry on. I don't know how much longer any of us can carry on. It was great

[37]

in the beginning, we were really getting somewhere. Not any longer.

MITCHELL: We're helping to keep ten million people from starving to death.

O'BRIEN: We feed them today and tomorrow they're hungry again. When is it ever going to stop? We can't beat the Nigerians and they can't beat us. It just goes on and on and on.

MITCHELL: You shouldn't push yourself so hard.

O'BRIEN: I've got to keep pushing or I'd drop. I've been supervising the loading at Uli and I haven't been in bed the last two nights. I'll have another two nights next week and the week after that and the week after that. When I do get to bed I can't sleep properly. All that tinned stuff is giving me ulcers and I'm getting headaches ever since I broke my glasses. And another filling came out of my teeth yesterday. Sorry for going on so but you asked me.

MITCHELL: Yes.

O'BRIEN: There was a rather odd thing happened on the road today. You know that barrier about ten miles back on the road—they usually raise it as soon as they see the Caritas sticker on the windscreen but this time they didn't so I had to stop. Then this young soldier came over to the car with a gun in his hand. When he got near I saw it wasn't a gun at all, it was only one of those wooden dummies they use for drilling with. And he had no boots, not even a pair of sandals, just his two bare feet. He came over and put his head in the window and he said: "Father, have you got anything to eat?" I said I hadn't but he just stood there so I hunted round the floor of the car and I found a bit of a dried fish and I handed it to him. He took it and said, "Thank you, Father," and then without any warning he started to cry. It was very embarrassing. He couldn't turn round because he didn't want the others to see him crying so he just stood there with his head in the window, big tears rolling down his cheeks on to his hands and on to the piece of fish. And then I started to cry. I don't know what came over me, I just couldn't help it. There we were, two grown men, weeping on each other's shoulders like a couple of infants. It was the most ridiculous thing you could imagine.

MITCHELL: And what happened then?

O'BRIEN: Nothing. I mean, he sort of pulled himself together and went back to the barrier and let me through. But I felt such an idiot.

MITCHELL: What you need is a holiday.

O'BRIEN: We all need a holiday.

MITCHELL: And I'm going to see you get it. You can get home easily enough through Sao Tomé and a month or two in Ireland would really set you up again.

O'BRIEN: It sounds great but there's too much to be done here.

MITCHELL: There may be but you're not going to do it. To be brutally frank, you're heading for a crack-up and you're heading for it fast.

O'BRIEN: Anyhow, you're due to get home leave before I am.

MITCHELL [*Vehemently*]: No, I'm all right where I am. I've got my own survival system and it works here. I've no guarantee it would work anywhere else. I don't really feel at home except in this place. I'll get to work on it tomorrow for you and see what I can swing. You go to bed now and get a good night's sleep.

O'BRIEN: O.K. Where's Cyprian with that coffee?

MITCHELL: Never mind about Cyprian and his coffee. This'll make you sleep much better. [*Pours whiskey into his glass.*]

O'BRIEN: Thanks. Stop. Good night, Joe.

MITCHELL: God bless, Tony.

[*O'Brien goes.*]

MITCHELL: Cyprian! [*He goes towards kitchen.*] Cyprian! [*There is no answer. Mitchell walks thoughtfully back, pours some more whiskey. Then he switches off the living room light and sits in his chair on the verandah. After a while a light comes up over the table and Bishop FitzMaurice is seen sitting there.*]

BISHOP: Come in. [*Mitchell jerks to attention and then goes to desk as before.*] Ah, Father Joe. I'm delighted to see you again. You're looking fit and well, yes indeed, fit and well. Sit down, sit down. Cigarette?

MITCHELL [*Sits*]: I don't smoke, thank you.

BISHOP: No, of course, I remember. Well, how did you enjoy

[39]

your little holiday? I'm sure Ballyhaunis must seem very quiet after Biafra.

MITCHELL: I wouldn't know. I don't come from Ballyhaunis.

BISHOP: Well, Castlebar or Claremorris or wherever you do come from. The main thing is that you needed a rest and deserved a rest and I hope you had a rest.

MITCHELL: I'm tired resting. I want to get back to work.

BISHOP: Of course you do, of course you do. You haven't changed a bit. And that's just what I wanted to talk to you about.

MITCHELL: When can I go back?

BISHOP: Back to Biafra, you mean?

MITCHELL: Where else?

BISHOP: Where else, indeed. As I always say, you can take the missionary out of Nigeria, but you can't take Nigeria out of the missionary. Rather neatly put, I think.

MITCHELL: Very.

BISHOP: Did I ever tell you about the first time I came to Abukaba?

MITCHELL: Yes.

BISHOP: That was long before there was a Cathedral or a bishop there. There was just a chapel built of corrugated iron and a market place. I was the first resident priest and they gave me a tremendous welcome. Banners, flags, women dancing, palm wine flowing, gifts of chickens and yams and coconuts. It went on all day. I was really touched. I felt, these people have really accepted me, I am really a part of Abukaba. I even began to worry how they were going to pay for the celebrations. I found out three days later when they sent me all the bills. But, as I always say, it's the thought that counts. What were we talking about?

MITCHELL: We were talking about my return to Biafra.

BISHOP: You were parish priest of Uzala, weren't you?

MITCHELL: Yes.

BISHOP: And young O'Brien took over when you went away.

MITCHELL: That's right.

BISHOP: And is doing a very good job, I hear.

MITCHELL: So I hear.

BISHOP: It would be a pity to disturb him.

[40]

MITCHELL: There are other parishes.

BISHOP: Not so many now, not so many. Every time the federal troops capture a village, we lose another mission. We have the same number of priests in an area that keeps getting smaller. So there's no point in sending anyone back, taking up space in one of our planes, unless he's really needed.

MITCHELLS Plenty of people take up space in your planes that aren't really needed.

BISHOP: It's not just the single trip. It's the whole question of keeping him supplied. An Irishman needs things a Biafran doesn't. To keep one missionary alive, five babies may have to die. We have to be sure that every priest and nun in there is really indispensable to the work. We can't sacrifice African lives in order to keep some unnecessary European supplied with tins of meat or condensed milk or anti-malaria tablets.

MITCHELL: Or bottles of whiskey.

BISHOP: I didn't say that.

MITCHELL: I was saving you the trouble.

BISHOP: I know how you feel. I know how I felt when I had to resign as Bishop of Abukaba but it had to be done. We go where we're needed, when we're needed, and as long as we're needed. Not a moment longer. It's part of the loneliness and part of the happiness of a priest's life. Where you are needed just now is here in Ireland. As one of the heroes of Biafra you can have an immense influence for good, especially among young people. In point of fact, we have just the job for you. There is a vacancy in our new Dublin college for a teacher of Latin.

MITCHELL: Latin!

BISHOP: Yes, I remember how good you always were at Latin. The language of Cicero, the language of Augustine, the language of Aquinas. The language which gives most perfect expression to rhetoric and to philosophy and to prayer. Latin brings us back to the roots of our civilization and of our religion. Now let me see. You will be doing your Leaving Certificate Examination next summer?

MITCHELL: Yes, Father.

BISHOP: And you're seventeen, eighteen?

MITCHELL: Eighteen next birthday.

[41]

BISHOP: A wonderful age, Mitchell, a wonderful age. Your life stretches before you like a smiling landscape, a thousand paths, an infinity of opportunities. And by the age of fifty you'll be all washed up, put out to grass, teaching a dead language, a bored schoolmaster standing in front of a bored class. Well, I won't keep you any longer, Mitchell. See you at Rugby practice. [*Stands and goes out.*]

MITCHELL: Wait! Wait!

[*But the bishop has gone. Mitchell goes shakily to pour himself another glass. The sound of a car pulling up is heard. Zachary comes in. He is wearing a black soutane with purple sash and a gold cross and chain.*]

MITCHELL: Zachary!

ZACHARY: Is everyone all right here?

MITCHELL: Yes. What's the matter?

ZACHARY: Where's Tony?

MITCHELL: He's in bed.

ZACHARY: Tony! [*He disappears into house and is heard shouting.*] Tony! Get up! [*He comes back into the living room.*]

MITCHELL: Can I ask what all this is about?

ZACHARY: Have you heard anything from the front?

MITCHELL: No. It seems to be very quiet at the moment. I didn't hear a single shot all day. But of course it's nearly five miles away.

[*O'Brien comes in wearing his shorts and pulling on his shirt.*]

ZACHARY: It was five miles away this morning. Tonight there is no front left any more.

O'BRIEN: What's that, Zach?

ZACHARY: The Nigerians have broken through all along the front and the fifth army is heading straight for Uzala.

MITCHELL: How far are they away?

ZACHARY: Maybe a mile, maybe less. They've halted for the night but they'll be here at first light in the morning.

O'BRIEN: Well, it had to come sooner or later. I'll just put on a few clothes and I'll be ready to go. [*He goes.*]

ZACHARY: Do you want to pack some things?

MITCHELL: I'm all right. We keep our bags packed all the time. Where will we go? I suppose they could take us in the mission at Abukaba.

[42]

ZACHARY: No, we'll go straight to Uli airstrip. With any luck you'll be out of the country by morning.

MITCHELL: Wait a minute, who said anything about getting out of the country?

ZACHARY: You'll have to leave Biafra. I can't guarantee your safety otherwise.

[*O'Brien returns, wearing soutane and carrying two cases, his own and Mitchell's.*]

O'BRIEN: Here's your bag, Joe. Where are we heading for? Abukaba?

MITCHELL: No, Uli. We have just been served with deportation orders by His Lordship the Bishop.

ZACHARY: I am not ordering you. I am advising you to go for your own good.

MITCHELL: "For your own good." It makes a nice variation. It sounds better than saying: "We don't need you any more. You've given us the best years of your life and built us up and made us what we are and now we don't need you any more. In fact, we prefer not to have you around, reminding us of how much we owe you, how you educated us and civilized us and coaxed us down out of the bloody trees. So for your own good, for your own safety, get your fat white arse out of here before it's shot off!"

ZACHARY: I don't think you quite understand the situation. They're not just advancing on this front, they're advancing on every front. By tomorrow evening the third and fifth armies will have joined up, the country will be split in two, and the airstrip will be cut off. Some time next day the surrender of Biafra will be announced. There is nothing that anyone can do to stop it.

MITCHELL: What about your great Biafran army, your famous one million fighting men?

ZACHARY: How much do you know about the Biafran army, Father, apart from what you hear on Biafra radio? Let me tell you about the Biafran army. In the Uzala sector, only one in three has a gun of any kind. Ammunition is being issued at the rate of five rounds per man per week. No new footwear has been available for more than six months. And for the last fortnight they have been getting one meal of

[43]

yams and garri every second day. Even the ordinary people know it's all over. If you were an Ibo, if you really knew the people and understood their language, you'd know it was the end of Biafra. If you don't believe me, go down to the village. The people have all gone—not along the road as refugees, but into the bush. Tomorrow when the army has moved in, they'll creep back to their houses and try to start life again as Nigerians, if they are let. Or if you don't believe me, ask Cyprian. That is, if he hasn't run into the bush himself.

O'BRIEN [*To Mitchell*]: We'll ask Cyprian, then.

MITCHELL: Cyprian isn't here. He's run away.

ZACHARY [*Lifts Mitchell's case*]: We'll go, Father. We have to collect Mother Gertrude at the convent.

MITCHELL: Does she know?

ZACHARY: Yes. She's getting ready. The Ibo sisters are going into the bush.

MITCHELL: What about the other missionaries?

ZACHARY: Most of them should be on the way to the airport by now.

MITCHELL: What about the ones who don't get away?

ZACHARY: I don't know. Some of them may get shot during the confusion. If they survive, they'll probably be put in prison and afterwards deported. So it's simpler to go now.

MITCHELL: You go, Tony, I'll stay.

O'BRIEN: What do you want to stay for?

MITCHELL: For one thing, the Bishop says he's not ordering us to go. For another thing, there are sixty kids in the school and twenty patients in the hospital who will have to be fed tomorrow and the day after until things get sorted out. And anyhow, I don't think all the missionaries should go. We've stuck with the people through the good times and the bad and I think we should stick with them to the end. Even if we're arrested or shot, they'll remember that some of us stayed.

O'BRIEN: If anyone is going to stay, I'll stay. I'm younger, I'm better able to look after myself.

MITCHELL: No, you can start work somewhere else, Kenya or Sierra Leone or Gambia—there's plenty of places. I'm too old to make a fresh start now.

[44]

O'BRIEN: Talk to him, Zach.

ZACHARY: He's right. It would be safer for him than for you. He's less likely to be mistaken for a mercenary.

MITCHELL: Then you don't mind if I stay?

ZACHARY: No, I don't mind. But from now on you're on your own.

MITCHELL: That's fair enough. God bless, Tony. Safe journey. [*Shakes hands.*]

O'BRIEN: Good-bye, Joe, mind yourself.

MITCHELL: Good-bye, Zachary. They won't shoot you, will they? [*Shakes hands.*]

ZACHARY: I don't think so. Not with bullets the price they are. Let us pray for each other.

MITCHELL: Will do.

[*They go. Mitchell potters restlessly around the room, takes up his case, puts it into a corner. He sips from his glass, then brings it out onto the verandah. He is barely seated when Bishop FitzMaurice appears again.*]

BISHOP: Come in.

MITCHELL: Drop dead!

BISHOP: Cigarette?

MITCHELL: If I've told you once, I've told you a thousand times . . . [*He goes over to table.*]

BISHOP: I'm sorry. I just thought you might appreciate some home comforts after doing your spell of penal servitude. I'm sure that life in an African prison has its moments of tedium. However, that's all over now and it's great to have you back in Ireland again. I was sorry I couldn't get out to meet you at Dublin airport but I had to go to a cocktail party at the Nigerian embassy. Very pleasant it was too, the word Biafra was never mentioned even once. But I'll have to learn to go easy on the smoked salmon. I hope you weren't expecting some kind of official welcome at the airport?

MITCHELL: The thought had crossed my mind.

BISHOP: You see, if you don't mind me saying so, you are just a tiny bit of an embarrassment at this stage. The war is well over now and the wounds are healing and no one wants unpleasant memories revived. You did a great job under conditions which are no longer relevant. Your name is written

[45]

in the Book of Life, there's no need to have it in the newspapers as well. You see, both the Congregation and the Irish Government think it is essential to let bygones be bygones and to strengthen our ties with the new Nigeria. I'm trying to work out a scheme whereby we can get young missionaries back into the country, teach them the language really well, get them to take out Nigerian citizenship, total identification.

MITCHELL: They'd still be white men.

BISHOP: They could get skin transplants.

MITCHELL [*Enraged*]: What kind of a fool are you trying to make out of me?

BISHOP [*Calmly*]: What kind of a fool are you trying to make out of yourself?

MITCHELL: You've never given me a chance. You've hated me all the time. You've been against me from the very beginning.

BISHOP: If I didn't exist, you would have had to invent me. In a way, you did invent me, making an evil genius out of a rather kind-hearted old gentleman. And you are inventing me now. A combination of paranoia and alcohol has me here, sitting behind this desk. I'm here because you want me here, because you want someone to blame beside yourself. Your life is one long succession of failures and mistakes, but it doesn't matter as long as you can blame me. You need me, you need to feel that I am responsible for everything that has gone wrong. I am the only security you've got.

MITCHELL: I don't need you, I don't need you. Go away! Get out!

BISHOP: Very good, I'll go. But I'll be back.

[*He stands up and walks out. Mitchell goes back to chair on verandah, trembling and breathing heavily. He makes the sign of the cross. Opens his breviary, is unable to concentrate, closes it again.*]

MITCHELL: O God, I can't pray, I can't read, I can't think. All I can do is sit here, as I've been sitting here for the past twenty-five years. There's got to be a meaning somewhere to all the pain and the failure, to the broken bodies and the starving children and the young nun lying in her own blood. If you can make any sense out of it, dear God, please let

[46]

me know, because I can't.

[*He sits a while motionless. Gradually the stage grows lighter as a new day begins to dawn. It becomes brighter and somewhere a cock crows. Mitchell rouses himself and takes a pace or two on the verandah. Then he hears someone approaching and he freezes. Mother Gertrude appears out of the morning mist and comes on to the verandah. She is carrying a suitcase and a basket.*]

GERTRUDE: Good morning, Father.

MITCHELL: What on earth are you doing here?

GERTRUDE: When the bishop told me you were staying, I decided to stay too. The idea of you looking after kwashi-orkor children! What would you give them?

MITCHELL [*Shrugs*]: Coffee?

GERTRUDE: Tchah! Still, it doesn't matter. I have all their diet sheets here.

MITCHELL: Why did you not go last night?

GERTRUDE: I never trusted that airlift from Uli. They're a real fly-by-night crowd, if you ask me. Anyhow, after all my time in Nigeria, I'm not going to sneak away in the dark. If they want to throw me out, they can look me in the eye while they're doing it. Would you like a cup of tea?

MITCHELL: Yes, I would.

[*She sits on one of the verandah chairs and opens the basket. She takes out flask, cups, sandwiches, milk, sugar. She pours out tea for the two of them. Meanwhile the conversation continues.*]

GERTRUDE: The other sisters got this ready before they left. They went just before dawn.

MITCHELL: Into the bush?

GERTRUDE: Yes, you never know with soldiers, especially if they get hold of drink. They'll come back in a day or two and carry on the work. It's just the transition that's awkward. I appointed Bibiana superior. I don't actually have the right to appoint anyone but this is no time for legalities. One lump or two?

MITCHELL: Two, please.

GERTRUDE: There's some sandwiches there but don't take one unless you intend to eat it all. We might need them later.

[47]

They cried a fair amount before they went and they said they'd pray for me always. I think Bibiana will be good, she's sensible and she gets on well with people. She said I should be safe enough and she didn't think there was much chance anyone would try to rape me.

MITCHELL: We must be thankful for small mercies.

GERTRUDE: I think I can understand why mothers cry at their daughters weddings. They don't need me any more. It doesn't matter now whether I live or die: they can carry on without me. I might have been a bit hard at times but they turned out all right. I know a lot of people laughed at me because I insisted on rules and regulations and because I always made the girls dress properly. But I made those girls respect themselves and I made others respect them. When I came to Uzala girls were being bought and sold like cattle. That doesn't happen now and please God it'll never happen again. They can do without you and me now and that means we did the job we came here to do. Another cup of tea?

MITCHELL: Don't touch that flask.

GERTRUDE: Why?

MITCHELL: Just stay the way you are, nice and calm and relaxed.

GERTRUDE: Is there someone coming?

MITCHELL: Yes.

GERTRUDE: I can't see without my glasses.

MITCHELL: It's a Nigerian soldier with an automatic rifle. He is coming right this way. Just sit where you are, don't make any sudden movements, he may be a bit nervous.

[*A soldier comes through the audience and on to the stage. He steps on to the verandah and points the gun at Mitchell.*]

SOLDIER: Stand up. [*Mitchell obeys.*] Put your hands up. Turn around. All right, you can sit down. [*To Gertrude.*] Now you stand up.

GERTRUDE: I will not. Who do you think you're talking to? What's your name? Where are you from?

MITCHELL: Mother, you'd better do what he says. He has a gun.

GERTRUDE: Well, what's your name?

SOLDIER: Gregory Olume.

GERTRUDE: And where do you come from?

SOLDIER: Calabar.

[48]

GERTRUDE: What school did you go to?

SOLDIER: Saint Fintan's.

GERTRUDE: Did you know Sister Laurence?

SOLDIER: Yes, sister. She taught me.

GERTRUDE: She didn't teach you much manners, did she?

SOLDIER: I am only obeying orders. We were told to beware of white mercenaries.

GERTRUDE: White mercenaries! I've been through the whole war and I've never even seen a white mercenary.

SOLDIER: Is there anyone else in the house?

MITCHELL: No, there's no one else here.

SOLDIER: You are a Catholic Father?

MITCHELL: Yes.

SOLDIER: And you are a Catholic Sister.

GERTRUDE: Yes. What are your orders about white missionaries?

SOLDIER: All white missionaries are to be put under immediate arrest and brought to Port Harcourt for trial.

GERTRUDE: Do you know that there are sixty children sick in the school and twenty patients in the clinic and if we are taken away there will be no one to look after them.

SOLDIER: Sister, I have to obey my orders.

GERTRUDE: If I refuse to go with you, will you shoot me?

SOLDIER: No, but my captain will shoot me.

MITCHELL: All right, Gregory, we'll go.

[*They stand to go. A noise is heard from inside the house.*]

SOLDIER: What is that? [*He runs into the living room.*] There's someone in the house. It is a trap. [*Swings gun wildly.*] Whoever you are, come out with your hands up or I fire.

[*Cyprian comes out with his hands up.*]

MITCHELL: Cyprian!

SOLDIER: You know him?

MITCHELL: Yes, it's Cyprian, our cook. I thought he had run away. You came back, Cyprian.

CYPRIAN: Yes, Father, I came back. I was afraid the children would die.

GERTRUDE: Cyprian, this is Gregory Olume, he has come to liberate us. You are all Nigerians now. You are brothers. Shake hands. [*Awkward pause.*] Don't be silly, Cyprian, you can't shake hands with them stuck in the air. [*They shake*

[49]

hands gingerly.] Now, this is the list of patients, with all special diets noted. You can report on their progress to Sister Bibiana when she gets back—Mother Bibiana, I should say. These are the keys of the dispensary and this one is for my office. The glass panel is a bit loose so don't slam the door. You know what to give the children.

CYPRIAN: Yes, Mother.

GERTRUDE: It will be hard work, but it's only for a day or two.

CYPRIAN: I will do it, Mother. They are my people.

GERTRUDE: Cyprian, I love you. [*To his surprise she kisses him on the cheek. She proceeds to pack the basket.*]

MITCHELL: Good-bye, Cyprian, and God keep you always.

CYPRIAN: Good-bye, Father. I will write you. [*They shake hands.*]

MITCHELL: You are still going to follow your aim?

CYPRIAN: Yes, Father.

MITCHELL: Relentlessly?

CYPRIAN: Mercilessly.

[*Mitchell takes the two cases, his and Gertrude's.*]

GERTRUDE [*To soldier*]: Well, what are we waiting for?

SOLDIER: What are we waiting for?

GERTRUDE: You don't expect me to carry that basket? A woman of my age?

[*The soldier hesitates, then takes the basket in his free hand. They go off, first Mitchell, then Gertrude, then the soldier. Cyprian looks after them, then sits on the step of the verandah and starts checking the diet sheets. A thought strikes him. He gets up, and quite casually sits in Mitchell's chair. He continues with his task of checking the list.*]

THE END.